Essex Trifles

by

Stan Jarvis

COUNTRYSIDE BOOKS

NEWBURY · BERKSHIRE

First published 1998
© Stan Jarvis 1998

COUNTRYSIDE BOOKS
3 Catherine Road
Newbury, Berkshire

ISBN 1 85306 513 7

Produced through MRM Associates Ltd., Reading
Printed by J. W. Arrowsmith Ltd., Bristol

CONTENTS

'Mind your head' was the cry when searching out some privies, as the author found here at Boreham.

FOREWORD

Let me take you back to 1951, when my dear wife and I grabbed the amazing chance to rent our first ever whole home – a primitive cottage on the coast. I thought that we must be the last people in England to have a privy, and to have to undertake those 'midnight burials' in order to dispose of the contents of that big bucket in all weathers. This included those summer nights when it never did seem dark enough to do the job discreetly. Research for this book has proved to both of us that we were very wrong.

We have been astonished to find so many people who could remember so clearly and explain so lucidly a way of life that we had thought quite dead by the beginning of the Second World War. When we began our search for privies actually still standing we did not realise how many people still held their 'sheds of relief' in such affectionate regard that they not only left them standing but also kept them in good repair. But for their kindness in writing their memories, providing photographs and drawings and allowing us the freedom of their back gardens to take our own pictures this book could not have been written.

In all honesty it would not have been written without the suggestion from, and the encouragement of, Nicholas Battle of Countryside Books. He made me see what a milestone had been passed when the privy came indoors as the 'toilet' and automatic flushing at the pull of a chain became totally taken for granted. Having served the public as a librarian for many years I have found in retirement that the spirit of 'What? Why? When?' was still strong in me and I was soon immersed in learned tomes on sanitation and social history. Subsequently, 27 newspapers and magazines covering Essex were kind enough to publish my plea for help, and 150 people took the trouble to write, telephone or visit me at home. Many were able to produce photographs. Their enthusiasm and interest, which I acknowledge with gratitude, enabled me to put together the following tribute to the memory of the good old Essex privy.

STAN JARVIS

Hedingham Castle – the garderobes were sited at the north-east corner of the keep.

[1]

PRIVY HISTORY

Human beings have been on earth through hundreds of thousands of years. They have persisted against all kinds of hazard and hardship, finding food and drink to stay alive and propagate their species. In doing so they have had to relieve themselves of the waste from solids and liquids passing through their digestive systems. For at least 450,000 years they urinated and defecated without concern for hygiene or modesty. Why and how humans became 'civilised' in their toilet habits can be followed up in volumes on social history. I shall, however, start you off on the path to the privy back in AD 1189.

That was when what we might call the first hygiene regulation was issued to govern the growing City of London. It included the proper construction and emptying of '. . . the necessary chambers [little rooms, or privies] in the houses of citizens.' There is another reference, in 1291, to 'common privies', forerunners of our 'public conveniences': in London, on its Essex border, John de Abingdon was murdered by a gang of roughs in the act of using such a privy. Bridges over the Thames were then very convenient structures on which to build privies because the excrement was allowed to drop straight into the river and be carried out to sea on the next ebbing tide. It was a Cockney observation at that time that London's bridges were built 'for wise men to go over and fools to go under' – boatmen had the odious task of shooting these bridges at their peril. In 1355 the Fleet river, where Fleet Street now runs, was stated to be choked with filth from no less than eleven privies built out over it and three sewers which discharged straight into it.

Such primitive privies existed in Essex right down to

relatively modern times. We know this from a report in the *Chelmsford Chronicle* for 29th October 1824, when the White Hart Inn at Brentwood had a 'bumby' or public cesspit in its yard. Such a riot broke out! Two men who were informing on Brentwood publicans so that they could claim a government bounty were cornered by a very angry crowd which assembled in that yard. The men were grabbed, knocked about and dragged through '. . . a filthy place in the White Hart Inn yard, by which they became truly objects of commiseration. Then they were captured from their police protectors again at the Fleece Inn at Brook Street. Here they were dragged through the horse-watering in front of the house, but they sustained no further injury than a sound ducking, and a beneficial cleaning of what they carried away from Mr. Wicks's bumby.'

From the earliest days monasteries provided 'lavers' or lavatories – stone troughs filled with water where the working brothers could clean themselves thoroughly before their evening meal. A.J. Lamb, reporting on excavations at the site of St Albans Abbey in 1924, tells us: 'Here was found a deep pit . . . the depth below the cloister floor level was 25 feet. At the bottom were found pieces of pottery and fragments of coarse cloth which, it is thought, were old gowns torn up by the monks and used as toilet paper' (paper of any kind was not made in Britain until late in the 15th century).

Another building of the Middle Ages which needed sanitary provision for its inmates was the castle with its keep. Good examples can be seen at Castle Hedingham and at Colchester. The name given to this type of privy is 'garderobe' – from the French – meaning not only a place where clothes were kept, a wardrobe, but also applied to the little room where clothing could be removed for the private act of defecation. Of Castle Hedingham Nikolaus Pevsner writes, 'In the thickness of the wall are divers narrow chambers or recesses. One of these, in the northeast angle, can be identified as a garderobe or lavatory.' Actually there are similar recesses on three floors, one above another and all connected by a shaft down which it would seem that the waste fell to a cesspit from which it could be shovelled into a cart and dumped in the moat, now but a dry ditch. Where a moat was not feasible in the construction of a castle the excrement was shot out of individual garderobes or down a main channel to rot away at the base of the wall.

By the time London's first major sanitary act was passed in 1358 many communal privies had been built to service tenement blocks, as we might call them, though there were still plenty of houses from which the contents of chamber pots were simply flung straight out of the bedroom windows. This constituted a considerable risk for unwary passers-by, though the emptier of the pot should have shouted the accepted warning 'Gardez loo!' (gardez-l'eau) – 'watch out for the water'.

Cesspits were less dangerous to the health and happiness of passers-by, but they had to be emptied regularly. For this purpose, in large centres of population, 'gongfermers', or mobile cleaners, were employed. There was no shortage of them because they could charge well for each collection, which might consist of months of accumulated ordure.

At the end of the 16th century Queen Elizabeth had a water closet invented by Sir John Harington – was that why he was knighted, I wonder? In 1596 he wrote a diatribe on the disgusting state of the nation's toilet habits, but succeeding monarchs down to James II carried on with their 'close stools', described by John Gloag in his *Short Dictionary of Furniture* as: 'An enclosed stool or box, containing a pewter or an earthenware vessel. Sometimes called a necessary stool or night stool ...' The name continued until the 19th century, when Victorian delicacy favoured the more general term 'night commode'. The famous cabinet-maker Sheraton wrote in 1803 that some night tables were made 'to imitate the appearance of a small lobby chest of drawers, having the top hinged behind, so that it may lift up to a perpendicular position.' Surely close stool and night table were the father and mother of the cottage privy, without the necessity for a midnight march up the garden path!

The water closet resurfaced in plans for houses drawn up from the 18th century onwards. It was not particularly popular but it did lead the way from the insanitary conditions then prevailing towards the continuing refinements.

John Booker, writing *Essex and the Industrial Revolution*, makes a good point. 'The drainage plans, complementary to the schemes for water supply, illustrate the birth pangs of the modern sanitary society at their most painful. It was a fact of life which the Victorians had to face that the disposal of waste and excreta in towns could no longer be left to chance or delegated to whoever was prepared to tender for its removal. The Chelmsford 'improving' Act of 1789 had delicately prevented the emptying of what it called 'Necessary Houses' in public places in the dead of night, but much stronger measures were patently needed in every urban community.' In Glebe Place, Chelmsford, as late as 1850 there was still just one privy used by all the inhabitants of seven houses. Even the better class houses on the main street of the town lacked proper privies or water closets.

There is evidence from as early as 1805 that the dung collected from Chelmsford's privies was subsequently sold. In 1842 another source reported that many Witham inhabitants kept their privy waste to sell it privately as manure. No doubt this was through the influence of J.J. Mecchi, a naturalised Italian who bought Tiptree Hall in 1840. By 1845 he had connected the outlets of his water closets to brick-built lakes where the excreta was mixed with chemicals and earth to produce fertiliser for his fields on a large scale. Mecchi campaigned for the use of more sewage and less imported fertilisers like guano, pointing out that John Morton, at Lodge Farm, Barking, was using many tons of London sewage on his fields with great success. Such schemes were far in advance of their time. It was not until 1876 that the Rivers Pollution Act at last put a stop to the piping of sewage direct into rivers. Ten years after that one could find a row of cottages in Hall Road, Heybridge, where all the excreta from eight privies drained directly into two great open cesspools immediately behind them. By 1858 Chelmsford's improved sewerage system was in full working order, though not yet involving every residence. The sewage drained through pipes laid underground to great tanks just off Lady Lane where the effluent was treated to remove its odour before it was released into the river below the town.

From the 18th century on, as public health and the causes of infection became better understood, the privy came into use, as a glorified chamber pot for all the family in its own little house, set apart in the back garden or communal passage. A certain amount of personal pride was demonstrated in its construction, size and situation, very much along the lines of the status symbol of a new car today.

The water closet was a natural development from the 'bucket-and-chuck-it' of the primitive privy. In 1775 Alexander Cummings, a London watchmaker, registered the first patent for an improved version of Sir John Harington's contraption. Cummings added the water trap – the bend at the bottom which retained water between the bowl and the outflow pipe to seal off the sewer and its smell. Yet it did not catch on – without a system of mass-production it was beyond the financial reach of most people. Joseph Bramah's design of 1778 was an important improvement in that the water, gravity fed, swirled round the bowl to clean it well with every flush. By 1800 he had sold some 6,000 water closets – one to every 1,333 people then alive in England! It required an efficient system of sewerage – with pipes to be laid underground, usually to the nearest river. That was why London's sewerage system over the next century was a disorganised disgrace. In 1854 research showed that cholera could be traced to a water supply fouled with human excrement, but official recognition of this problem was delayed for what was termed as lack of sufficient evidence. When the germ causing cholera was isolated in 1883 the point was proved and then the rush to install flush lavatories began.

In the populous districts of Essex on its London borders, it was the poor who continued to suffer the diseases and death brought about by crowded living conditions in tenements, but there were unhygienic slums in the so-called cottages further out in the country districts. Where they had space these cottagers could at least erect a privy, and empty the large family bucket into a conveniently dug pit in the garden, whereas in the close-built town tenements a part of a room was given up to the privy with a pit dug through to the foundations with a seat over it. The excrement was emptied once it had filled the pit. Later the 'gongfermers', now called 'nightmen', collected the buckets which were left out for them and emptied them into a cart. For the upper storeys in those tenements the old chamber pots were kept in service or the privy bucket was lugged down the stairs on 'collection' day. In New Street, right in the centre of Chelmsford, there were several cesspits under the ground floor of cottages just as they had been since Tudor times.

In 1846 the public health revolution was under way with the passing of the first Public Baths and Wash Houses Act. In that same year Doulton's famous pottery at Lambeth began the manufacture of stone-glazed pipes, the first necessity of an efficient system for the disposal of sewage entirely divorced from the provision of water for other domestic requirements.

In 1848 the very first Public Health Act for Britain came into force as the result of a serious outbreak of cholera which greatly affected the vast conurbation of London. A Board of Commissioners took over the unified control of sewage disposal in London from eight different local authorities. The Act included regulations which separated those rivers from which water was drawn for human consumption and those used to carry away the effluent from the sewers.

Three men, who one historian called 'The Three Musketeers of Plumbing' were waiting in the wings to complete the drama of this great revolution in public health. One was George Jennings whose siphonic wash-down of the new lavatory bowls gave greater cleaning force. The second was Thomas Crapper who was responsible for the chain we all pulled until quite recent times which operated a valveless cistern, thus reducing both the amount of water needed at each flushing and the noise made by the system as a whole. So effective was his work on the general health of the nation that he was knighted by Queen Victoria. His name has, of course, passed permanently into our language. The third 'musketeer', Thomas Twyford, produced a porcelain bowl and cistern. Thus, incidentally, he brought art into the water closet, with pedestals moulded with flowers and fruit in glorious colour.

It remained for the soil pipes and sewers to meet the flair and design of these three men. The man of the moment in this department was Edwin Chadwick who published in 1842 his seminal report on 'Sanitary Conditions of the Labouring Classes in Great Britain'.

Jennings was the instigator, at the opening of the 20th century, of the 'wash-down' urinals for men as well as the

Thomas Crapper's success enabled him to open showrooms in King's Road, Chelsea.

high-class toilets for both sexes provided under the street in large towns. It was Shanks who developed Jennings' invention, and his name still appears on sanitary bowls and wall fittings throughout the land.

Yet, despite all this action to protect the health of and provide modern amenities for the teeming masses on Essex's border with London and the people in the larger towns of the county, the simple privy carried on in all the semi-rural to totally isolated areas. It was considered a feature of life sufficiently important to be marked in proper scale on the 25 inches to the mile Ordnance Survey maps published around 1875. Privies like this persisted in such numbers, not only in Essex but throughout Britain, that the *Home-lovers Encyclopaedia for Handyman and Housewife*, published as late as 1934, still gives advice on the subject: '. . . the old types known as privy middens and privies are thoroughly insanitary and should be abolished, as the material is never completely or rapidly removed, and is not protected from flies, etc. Earth closets and pail closets are far less objectionable and can be made reasonably sanitary if emptied frequently, at least twice a week, and kept scrupulously clean. The material should be dug into trenches well away from the house or any source of water supply and should be covered with at least four inches of earth . . . The outbuilding for an earth closet can advantageously be built of brickwork and should be frequently lime-washed. A weatherboarded erection is cheaper, but the numerous crevices harbour a great number of insects. The floor should be of concrete raised to three inches above the level of the ground, with a fall to the entrance door. The cheapness of the best earth closet is a recommendation and if properly constructed it will prove satisfactory . . .'

15

lead-in is joined to the ...
of the switch. One side of the switch is thus
connected via the lead-in insulator to the aerial
terminal of the set, and the remaining side is
joined to earth. Thus in one position of the switch
arm the aerial is connected to the receiver, while
in the other position the aerial is joined direct to
earth. The aerial should always be earthed when
the set is not in use.

EARTH CLOSET. In country districts where
no public sanitary arrangements exist, an earth
or chemical closet, located in an outbuilding,
takes the place of the town water closet. A
simple form consists of a movable receptacle or
pail beneath the seat. Dry loamy earth may be
provided in a receptacle above the seat, feeding
through a hopper to a shoot terminating above
the pail at the back. A flap can be fitted to
regulate the flow of dried earth, as shown in the
figure below.

The outbuilding for an earth closet can advantageously be built of brickwork and should be
frequently lime-washed. A weatherboarded
erection is cheaper, but the numerous crevices
harbour a great number of
insects. The floor

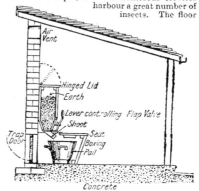

Earth Closet. Sectional diagram showing method of
Construction and hopper for earth supply

should be of concrete raised three inches above the
level of the ground, with a fall to the entrance
door. The cheapness of the best earth closet
system is a recommendation, and if properly constructed it will prove satisfactory.

It should be noted that dry loamy earth is
the best material, as its deodorant properties are
greater than those of ashes, etc. In fact, unless
earth be used, the closet may be treated by local
by-laws as a privy, with the result that more
frequent cleansing is insisted upon. This applies
particularly when a fixed receptacle is used.
See Cesspool ; Refuse ; Sanitation ; Water Closet.

EARTHENWARE. This term is used for
household and other articles made of clay and
similar substances. Glazed and unglazed earthenware of fireproof quality is largely used as a

The *Home-lovers Encyclopaedia for Handyman and Housewife* gave some useful
advice for privy builders.

16

[2]

A Beautiful Sight

Why were Essex privies built of wood with only the occasional building carried out in brick? The answer is that in medieval times the area was covered by a great forest of which Epping and Hatfield forest are only the miniscule remains. So when the time came to meet the modern responsibilities of sewage disposal in the interest of public health Essex man turned to the forest to cut timber for his backyard privy, and wood continued to be used as the principal material right down to the present century.

The privy building was always of simple construction and easily repaired. It also had to be designed with the user, or users, in mind – either with several seats (sometimes as many as six or seven) for groups of people such as farm workers, or with just a single seat to accommodate the needs of a cottager. Families needed more than one seat, with sizes varied to suit adults and children. Large numbers of new privies were built during the 19th century to meet the continuing expansion of the population and there are many examples to be seen in Essex today, although none, as far as I know, are still in use. Even more were built by amateurs in modern times, when East Enders seized the chance, during more than one agricultural depression, to buy their own bit of land on the old 'plotlands' where Basildon now sprawls proudly as a new town. They found weekend escape from the mean streets of the 'great wen' of London, as William Cobbett called it in 1821.

The do-it-yourself builder of the privy on his plot was basically guided by the dimensions of the human beings who would use it. For example, the height had to be sufficient for a six-foot man, the width had to allow access for the fattest in

A standard Essex privy with seat and bucket – found at Hatfield Broad Oak.

A tiled wooden privy in Hempstead.

the family, and the depth had to allow any adult to sit down in comfort and attend to themselves when they had finished. So the woodwork at the back of the privy had to be ruggedly strong, particularly if including more than one seat, and sufficiently supported all the way across over the buckets or the pit. For decency's sake the front was filled in with a panel which might include hinged doors or flaps to allow removal of the buckets for emptying. An alternative was to have a door at the back of the privy, behind the seat, so that the buckets could be removed more discreetly. Such variations would depend on the situation of the privy and the decision of the builder on the method for disposal of the ordure.

Most single privies were of the 'bucket-and-chuck-it' kind, where a hole was dug in the garden well away from the house and privy and the contents of the bucket were buried some two feet or more below the surface – the site for the digging being continually circulated around the garden. But there were many terraced houses, in both town and country, where space was saved and servicing made easier by incorporating a

A pair of wooden privies, used up until the early 1970s in Gosfield.

cesspit, which would be excavated in the ground under the seats of two or more privies and extended along the backs. It would be covered inside by the privy seats, which had wooden covers placed over the holes, and outside by boarding or corrugated iron which could be lifted periodically to allow the digging out of the ordure using a large, long-handled scoop. This would then be loaded onto a cart for disposal at a designated local dump, thrown onto a farmer's fields, or slid into a handy river for dispersal by the current.

The privy door was often pierced decoratively, or the top or bottom cut off to allow ventilation – most necessary in summer. The roof was often of a single pitch, like a lean-to. Sometimes, however, it descended from the centre to each side, giving the privy very much the appearance of a wide sentry box.

One likes to think that many Essex privies were built with the same pride and skill that was displayed by Lem Putt, the

A rural idyll in Layer-de-la-Haye? One of Rye Farm's former privies can be seen under the spreading tree in the centre.

21

champion privy builder of Sangamon County, as described in Charles Sale's marvellous little book, *The Specialist*, which gave such good advice to the pioneer in the New Country: 'Now, about the diggin' of her. You can't be too careful about that . . . dig her deep and dig her wide. It's a mighty sight better to have a little privy over a big hole than a big privy over a little hole . . . I can give you a lean-to type or a pitch roof. Pitch roofs cost a little more, but some of our best people have lean-tos . . . I'll tell you why.

'A lean-to has less corners for the wasps to build their nests in; and on a hot August afternoon there ain't nothing so disconcertin' as a lot of wasps buzzin' 'round while you're settin' there doing' a little readin', figgerin', or thinkin' . . .

'. . . Now, about ventilators, or the designs I cut in the doors. I can give you stars, diamonds, or crescents – there ain't much choice – all give good service . . . I do cut twinin' hearts now and then for young married couples; and bunches of grapes for the newly rich.'

Lem then talks at great length about the door. It should be

Two-seater at Stubbard Farm, Pleshey. (Photograph courtesy of Charles Stock)

looked at from the sitter's point of view. A door opened half inwards gives air and sunshine – if you hear anybody approaching you can kick it closed with your foot and shoot home the bolt. If that door opened outwards just imagine the difficulty you'd be in!

Lem goes on to give a tip about painting the privy: '. . . If I was you, I'd paint her a bright red, with white trimmin's – just like your barn. Then she'll match up nice in the daytime, and you can spot 'er easy at night, when you ain't got much time to go scoutin' around.' Then he concludes: 'There's a lot of fine points to puttin' up a first-class privy that the average man don't think about. It's no job for an amachoor, take my word on it. There's a whole lot more to it than you can see by just takin' a few squints at your nabor's.'

And when the successful privy builder has finished his handiwork he can allow himself to '. . . jest sit there lookin' at that beautiful sight. There sits that privy on that knoll near the wood-pile, painted red and white, mornin' glories growin' up over her and Mr. Sun bathin' her in a burst of yeller color as he drops back of them hills . . . As I look at that beautiful picture of my work, I'm proud . . .'

But what, I wonder, would Lem Putt have made of Dennis Widdick's wartime memory? 'When the RAF were stationed at Rivenhall Airfield they dumped all their rubbish in some old sandpits opposite our house. As kids we used to rummage through it. One day we found a load of packing cases made of very thick cardboard. I told my uncle and we brought home a load, to use it as insulation for the inside walls of the toilet and distempered them to make our little hut look quite smart.'

[3]

PLOTLANDS REVISITED

Lavatory life on Essex plotlands is brought vividly to mind by
Mr Warren from Hullbridge, with his own potted history:

1929. Our 'loo', 'lavvy', 'karsi', 'bumby', 'dunnekin', 'WC'
(but *never* 'toilet') built on plot of land that my Dad bought
for £10. Size: 3 x 4 ft, 7 ft high, tongued and grooved timber
on concrete base. Simple seat across with heart-shaped hole,
big galvanised lavatory bucket. Close to the hedge a long
trench was dug for the 'bucket-and chuck-it' operation. Mum
insisted on Izal medicated paper. In the absence of a chain to
pull (no mains supply) a handful of hay and a sprinkle of
lime kept things tidy until it was time to empty. Wellies
needed for the long, muddy path through the wet grass while
we lived in a bell tent. A yearly coat of creosote has preserved
it to the present day. (That was my job.)
1936. Moved closer to the small bungalow that was built, with
a concrete path from the back door. Marvellous crop of
tomato plants lining the hedge.
1940. Family evacuate from London, so 'loo' working at full
capacity.
1946 (about). Chemical toilet installed, so seat burnt on Guy
Fawkes Night, and bucket used to force rhubarb. New
plywood and felt roof fitted to stop leaks. A blackthorn bush,
growing at the side, threatens to tilt it, so has to be chopped
down. So it starts to lean the other way and needs the present
long prop and an elderberry tree to hold it up straight, so the
door can open.
1985. I retire, to live here permanently, so have bathroom
and toilet fitted in bungalow. The old lav. is jammed-packed
with old junk and will stand for a good few years yet.

Mr Warren's privy in honourable retirement at Hullbridge.

Mrs Coomber, now of South Benfleet, was born in Dunton plotlands '. . . and like thousands of others we had no water, electric, etc. My father built his own bungalow and outside toilet, then, when my sister and I came along, he built a small one alongside, to the amusement of all our visitors.'

Mrs Manley was one of a family of nine who lived in a plotlands bungalow in Laindon, with absolutely no facilities. She recalls: 'The "privy", "carsey", "bog" was a small wooden shed affair, a good walk down the garden, behind an apple tree. It had no lighting which made it spooky on a moonlit night. During the dark hours we always went there in pairs. The girls would call on a brother to escort them. Many a time he would get fed up with waiting – "Haven't you finished yet?" he would call out. In winter it was dreadful.

'Inside the privy looked quite homely with a rag rug on the

floor. The lawn mower was kept in one corner and in the other was a wooden box. In it during the summer fresh grass cuttings were kept and sprinkled in the bucket to deter the flies.'

Mr Colin Findlay of Wickford sums up the nostalgia of old privy users: 'In 1931 my grandmother purchased a 'plotlands' bungalow in Basildon – a little-known country retreat for East Enders. This was my first introduction to the hole in the board with the bucket under.

'The structure, in timber, was halfway down the garden, amidst the fruit trees and vegetables. Paper was provided by a telephone directory threaded on string through one corner. When the bucket was full it was emptied into a trench which was filled in again and eventually grew fine marrows.

'In 1941 our family moved to the bungalow, having been bombed out in Forest Gate in the East End. The privy came under great pressure, for there were nine of us living in the bungalow and sleeping in an Anderson shelter – conveniently placed very near the toilet, from which, many a time, I watched the Battle of Britain being fought out in the skies. It was with great regret, in the early 50s, that our privy was included in compulsory purchase of land by the Basildon Development Council to provide more homes in the area of the New Town.

'Although I have travelled around the world and seen many other outhouse bogs none were ever so dear to me as our plotlands privy.'

[4]

THOSE WERE THE DAYS

Despite the ever-increasing lines of drainage pipes wriggling like worms through the earth beneath all the urban areas and smaller places within reach of rivers and the sea, many inhabitants of rural Essex had to make do with their primitive privies well into the twentieth century.

Mr C. Balm recalls: 'I lived in Wivenhoe as a lad from 1919 until 1928 before coming to Ingatestone. I well remember our house, built about 1900, had an outside "earth closet" as my parents described it. The toilet was brick built and attached to the house, we had to go out of the back door and round the corner to get to it, it had a wooden seat the same width as the closet with a hole in the centre to suit most "bottoms" and a pail beneath. There was a small door in the brickwork at the side of the closet just large enough for the pail to be withdrawn. The pails were emptied at night, about 1 or 2 am by council men who carried them on their shoulders round the house to empty them into a specially made cylindrical iron cart drawn by a horse. This routine was repeated at each house in the road.'

It is amazing to think that a privy identical to those being used from the 16th century was still in use in Elsenham right down to our day. Gordon Barker, who sent a photograph of the privy – in Robin Hood Road – taken in 1986, remarks, 'Our family used such a privy until 1956 and when we sat in there we didn't know where the wind was coming from, but we knew where it was going!'

Mrs Edwards of Brentwood recalls her childhood in a cottage in Coxtie Green: 'Of course we'd have to visit the privy in all weathers and get soaked in the pouring rain and freeze with the cold in the winter. We always had to take a

J. Henry Powter outside his privy, the last one surviving in Elsenham. Taken after a heavy snowfall in February 1986.

bucket of water to tip down the pan as there was no flush. During the war when it was difficult to get toilet rolls my father would cut newspaper up in squares and, making a small hole in one corner of a pile of thirty or so, he would thread a piece of string through the hole and hang it on a nail on the door, which, incidentally, had a peep-hole in, because a knot in the wood had come out – one way of knowing if someone was in there if one needed the privy!

'At one time, when my mother catered for teas, she would often have cyclists or ramblers queuing up along the path for their turn to use the privy.'

Mrs Maureen Barker of Braintree gives us a child's-eye view of her introduction to a privy, the 'little shed': 'You can imagine how I felt trying to perch myself on this large wooden seat and trying to keep my balance over that "large" hole in it. My great-uncle had rigged up a small shelf so, as dusk fell a "night-light" was placed on it. You can understand that with eight people using it the container filled up pretty quick, so neighbours kindly let us use theirs. The containers were only emptied once a week, in the early hours of the morning, into a cart which came round. Gosh! it's hard to realise these places existed, a haven for bluebottles. My great-aunt kept the wooden seat white almost with her scrubbing of soap and water and the old Jeyes Fluid – not much else to combat flies and odours in those days.'

Mrs Burch, also of Braintree, now over 75, has some very personal memories too: 'Yes, I can tell you a few things about "privies" up the garden – best place for them when there was no plumbing . . . at the age of nine I moved from a house in Witham with modern plumbing to a farm miles away in the Essex countryside, where my father had been made foreman. There were five of us children aged from two to eleven. Our "toilet" was a square wooden box which concealed a strange-shaped pail with a heart-shaped hole for your bum and a wooden cover with a wooden handle like a cross. Even now I

'We were on the main road to Colchester, so everyone could see you take a trip to the little hut when they were waiting for the bus . . .' Dennis Widdick's childhood privy at the old cottages at Bridge Hall, Bradwell-juxta-Coggeshall.

remember always placing a piece of newspaper on top of what was already there before I sat down. Every few days it disappeared like magic, there was no cesspool, so it must have been buried. I have wondered since what happened when the ground was frozen. I remember my mother pouring a brown liquid into hot water which made it look like milk and scrubbing the seat with it, so once a week at least it used to smell nice.

'When I read a notice in the toilets of today: "Now wash your hands", I think chance would have been a fine thing because our water came from a running fresh spring which had to be carried in pails.'

'I can remember our outside loo with great clarity', says Mrs Nash of Harlow. 'The old privy had a wooden seat, scrubbed clean with carbolic and the stone front was whitened with whitening stone. Under the door was usually a gap of 4-6 inches and on cold, windy days you did not linger long; though my father would often take a newspaper with him and stay quite a while – but perhaps it was the only quiet place with six children in the house. I can see him now with his wide leather belt and braces holding his trousers up and newspaper tucked under his arm.'

Mr Rawlingson goes back seventy years on recollecting the privy at the back of his parents' cottage on Dukes Farm,

'I can see him now . . .' J. Henry Foster's picture of a dad in search of a quiet place to read.

Springfield: 'The privy was a shed-like construction similar to those one used to see on allotments for gardeners to house their tools. It was about six feet six inches tall with floor dimensions about three feet square. On opening the door one saw the toilet seat – a solid plank about eighteen inches wide fitted wall to wall. There was a hole about ten inches in diameter with a wooden lid which may have come from the end of a barrel. Underneath it was the traditional bucket . . . access to remove it was via a horizontally hinged door at the back of the "hut". This could be dangerous if jokers were about (bums could be stung with nettles!). The contents when removed were buried in the cornfield behind the house. In the spring we kids knew where, because the corn was always more lush there.'

At Bradfield, near Manningtree, Mr Wilson remembers, 'The lavatory was about 25 yards from our back door, it was sort of tall and square, creosoted outside, streaked with cream distemper put on liberally by Mum inside, using too much water. Sometimes it was blue when a change was reckoned. The door had "T" hinges and it was opened from

The old brick and tile privy at Ebenezer Cottage, Boreham, stands in the shadow of St Andrew's church (*opposite*). Note the three ventilation holes in its pediment.

the outside by lifting a straight iron latch, and from the inside by pushing your finger through the latch hole and pushing up the same straight catch on the outside.

'There were ventilator holes roughly cut in the top of the door. Other people's lavs had a wooden grating over the door, ours hadn't – the shiplap walls let in plenty of draught and you didn't stay very long on a rough winter's night.'

Sylvia Wade told me of the days of her childhood in the 'twenties when her grandparents were the tenants of the Red Lion in Sturmer up on the border with Suffolk: 'We would go for the Christmas every year. I was little and the privy was quite a walk down the garden. It was a wooden hut with a sneck latch on the door, a white wood, well-scrubbed bench seat with the necessary hole in it over the large bucket it concealed. If you needed to go after dark you took a candle to light when you got there. All very spooky and spidery! The bucket was emptied into the cesspit further down the garden. My grandad reckoned he had the best tomatoes around!'

Mrs Palmer of Hutton remembered privies at home and at work: 'When I was about four years old our privy stood well away from the house. I was always frightened to go in it not only because of the creepy crawlies that lurked about but also because the seat used to seem so large that I feared falling down into the horrible bucket. When I was about six we moved to a larger house but it still had a privy halfway up the garden, timber-built, with a trapdoor at the back so that the galvanised bucket could be pulled out when it needed emptying. It was quite a performance going to the loo in bad weather, putting on wellington boots and a coat.

'In 1951 I came to live in Shenfield and to work in a small "factory" unit – a building of brick with four toilets each for men and women. The "mens'" still had buckets which council men emptied each week. Thank God for today's modern living with loos indoors **and** central heating!'

Mrs Powell, born in 1921 in Abbeygate Street, Colchester, was four when the family moved from no 8 to no 18: '. . . our only toilet was at the end of the garden. It had a wooden seat with a hole for the toilet – we even had a cistern operated by a chain pull. The bench seat was very handy for putting a candle on when you went in the dark. This I hated as the candle flickered and cast shadows and I was quite a nervous child, scared stiff of spiders, although I cannot remember ever seeing any there.

'We had potties in the bedrooms and my parents had an enamel pail into which the pots were emptied. My brothers and I took turns in emptying this pail into the lav. I don't ever remember any resentment over having to do this. When I was old enough I had the job of scrubbing the wooden seat, which I quite enjoyed, and got very annoyed if anyone dropped candlegrease on it.'

Dick Wilkins of Rayleigh gives a clear account of before the last war when he was living at Eastwood where '. . . We had the usual outside privy, which consisted of a wooden seat with the necessary hole in the centre, fixed across two beams which ran the full width of a wooden hut three feet square and six feet high. Beneath the hole in the seat a large bucket was placed, being pushed in from the front. These buckets were specially made for this job, having one large handle for lifting, and another fixed to the side for emptying. They held about five gallons.'

Mrs Chipperfield of Goldhanger raises a smile with her privy memories: 'My great-aunt used to cut out gaily coloured pictures from magazines – animals, birds, flowers, scenery, babies and so on – and paste them on the walls like some enormous collage. There was a choice of paper – a proper toilet roll or cut up squares of newspaper threaded on a string. There was a wooden box on the floor filled with ash, plus a small shovel – when one had done a "Big Job" a little ash was used to conceal it.'

A privy that has kept up with the times at Southminster. The rugged and typically Essex weatherboarded exterior reveals, when the door is opened, a whitewashed interior with an up-to-date pedestal pan and shiny seat. It's a bit like the old and treasured retainer still offering his services to the family in the Big House. (Photograph courtesy of Theresa Cassels)

Angela Parker remembers . . .

Angela Parker of Althorne recalls: 'As a child in the 1950s, and with no main sewerage, we shared as a family the joys of the outside privy. My earliest memories are of a little shed, halfway down the garden and which to me, as a child, was a really creepy place. Earwigs and woodlice jostled for space with spiders, **big** spiders, and the only light came in through the half dozen holes bored in the top of the door.

'Nana's privy, on the other hand, was different. Hers had

ivy growing in it and even more spiders, but always seemed a quiet and peaceful place to sit and reflect. It had a spy-hole in the side so I could watch passers-by in the lane, and, as she bought the *Radio Times* there was always something interesting to read in the squares hanging on a string.

'Nana didn't have to empty her bucket because a lorry came every Thursday and took away the waste. I had to stay indoors on "Lavatory Day" as it wasn't considered "nice" to see the men collecting and I can remember feeling really sorry for those who earned their living in this way. Nana refused to be modernised and used her privy until the late 1970s.'

'I was born in the same cottage as my mother, on the corner of Mulberry Green, opposite the Green Man, Old Harlow,' writes Norah Day. 'I was born in 1919 and until I was about five years old we had oil lamps. Our next door neighbour shared the same building, with our "lavs" being back-to-back. Opposite our "lav" we had a greenhouse which we looked straight into if we kept the door open. In the "lav" we kept a bucket of water ready to put down the pan to flush it into the cesspit. A water butt was handy for the water but we also had a tap in the garden.

'Our winters were the most memorable time of year, walking up the garden in the dark, cold and sometimes wet nights, just a candle to see by. Previous to my birth my grandmother, who lived with us, lost a son of 18 years to typhoid, contracted from cleaning out the sewer pipe which stuck out from the earth in the garden. When I was 12 or 13 my father had a proper toilet installed. It was something beyond our wildest dreams to have a modern toilet with a flush cistern.'

Mrs Joan Wardle of Martello Bay, Clacton, remembers the days when she was little Joan Wright, living with her Mum and Dad 'in one of the three weatherboarded terraced cottages in Spring Road, St Osyth. Two up and two down with

Over 100 years ago Mrs Norah Day's grandparents posed for the camera in their back garden at Old Harlow. Their privy, adjoining their neighbour's, is in the background.

an outside tap between the three cottages the only source of water.

'The path to the lavatory went between our garden on the right and our neighbour's garden on the left, past the neighbour's long shed, then on to a path which ran behind it to three lavatories in a row, a wooden structure, all in one, with just a partition between each. So one tended to try and make sure no-one was in the next lav when you went, as you could hear all that was going on. I know I found it very embarrassing as a child, and kept quite still until they had gone, especially if it was a he.

'We were very lucky that the landlady was very enlightened (though she wouldn't have electricity put in the cottages until about 1938) so we had what you might call "flush" lavatories, unlike most people who had the wooden seat with the container underneath which had to be emptied. Not "flush" as we know it today! We had to take an enamel pail of water from the outside tap, past the next-door neighbour's door, to take with us to "flush", so everyone knew where we were going.

'When we went for the walk in the dark we used to have a "flash-lite". I was the proud owner of one of my own, a flat square with a big bulb at the front which also served as my light in the lavatory.

'When we left the cottage in 1940 due to the invasion threat, to go to my mother's people in Warwickshire, things were still the same as I have described. The cottages are still there now, as they are second-grade listed, but, of course, have now been made into one-bedroom properties, with all mod-cons.'

Mrs Marilyn Powling, born in 1945, was brought up in a small wooden bungalow in a road which no longer exists, all bulldozed away to make the main road from Langdon Hills to Basildon. Their privy, also wooden, was at the bottom of the garden, shielded from view behind a trellis of pink

Joan Wardle and her grandfather – complete with enamel pail after a 'walk up the garden' – at her childhood home in Spring Road, St Osyth.

climbing roses. Every year it was given a fresh coat of paint within, depending on what colour had been left over from decorating the house.

'It had a corrugated iron roof, how the rain sounded on it! Ours was a very long garden backing onto the railway and the privy was right at the end, a long walk in bad weather. When it snowed I had to don wellingtons to trek down there. There was always an umbrella left by the back door for when it rained.

'I'm married now and live in Dunmow and my lovely house has three indoor toilets and two bathrooms. What I find surprising when I look back is that we never had any food poisoning or tummy bugs. It just may be that the primitive conditions in which we lived caused us to build up a resistance in our bodies.'

FROM PIT TO FLUSH

Len Wyatt of Great Wakering bestrides a century of privy development, and is another who gives the precise measurements which are so valuable to historians. He was born in the cottage in which he still lives and his privy remains – though put to other purposes – at the bottom of the garden, '. . . not a very nice walk for us six children on a winter's night, especially when the candle blew out. At first our privy was just a deep pit regularly covered with earth. The seat, box-like, stretched the width of the building, with a neat hole cut in the top. Later the pit was filled in and a large bucket was put inside the box.

'The "Okey Okey" cart which came to empty it was a horse-drawn, half-round tank, like those used on farms for carting water. The "night men" used to bring their pails round and collect the contents of ours on a Friday night making a lot of noise with the clanking of the pails and all the dogs in the

Len Wyatt's old privy at Great Wakering. Still at the bottom of the garden, though now put to other purposes.

neighbourhood barking away. Us boys used to call it "Amami night" because Friday night was hair-washing night, using the well-known brand of shampoo.

'Most of the privies about Great Wakering had a "tea tree" set against them because it was reckoned to take all the odour way. Our privy was 80 feet from the back door, down a brick path. It was built back-to-back with the neighbours' under a pitched, slate-tiled roof. Measurements: width 50 inches, depth 50 inches, height to eaves 76 inches, with a door made from tongued and grooved planks 27 inches wide and 70 inches high.

'The outside toilet was built onto the back of the house just after 1930, when the sewage and water pipes were connected. This brick building with a high-level flush is still in use.'

. . . BUT WE MANAGED

Mrs Adams, of Chelmsford, now in her seventies, has remembered the privy in a very down-to-earth account: 'The house in which I was born had a wash-house a short distance from the back door. Built on the back of this was the toilet. There was no earth bucket but a shallow brick-built container with a wooden lid. This had to be emptied every so often. My father had to dig a deep hole in the garden for this. It was not very pleasant and we were kept in the house with doors and windows shut tight, Then, in later years, it was replaced with a bucket under the seat. This, of course, had to be emptied pretty often as there were six of us children. We didn't like our visits outside on a cold winter's night, but we managed.' Surely a typically British understatement?

[5]

SOME THOUGHTS ON PAPER

'When I went to stay with my aunt,' recalls Mrs Burch of Braintree, 'Saturday evenings were given over to cutting newspapers into squares and threading them onto binder string to hang in the privy; then when you went to use it you would tear off a piece with perhaps Pip, Squeak and Wilfred on, or something similar, then you would hunt for the connecting piece but you never could find the ending!'

Dick Wilkins remembers the days before toilet rolls in pre-war Eastwood: 'We made good use of the *Southend Standard* which was made of softer paper than most. It was torn into sheets about six by four inches which were stacked together and a red hot poker was then used to bore a hole through the top corner and thread them together on a loop of string which was then hung on a nail immediately to hand on the toilet wall.'

Miss Joslin, now in her nineties, has vivid memories of her years as a Home Help Organiser in the county. On one visit to an old cottager she found him busy cutting up newspaper into small squares. 'I asked him, "What are you doing?" He just quietly said, "Oh, bum fodder." Then he made small holes in each piece in the corner and threaded a piece of string through, to be hung on a nail on the wall in the "little house". He then said one must be careful to choose the right paper as some print comes off!'

Mrs D. Ritchie describes her childhood privy at the school house in Rettendon in the 1920s: 'The "Toilet Paper" hung on a string over a nail in the wall and if you were lucky was

45

The *Daily Mail* was always very popular . . .

the soft tissue type of paper in which all oranges were wrapped. There were pictures of the places from which they came. We always had plenty of oranges so the papers were smoothed and kept for this very useful purpose. The alternative – sheets of newspaper torn into appropriate sizes – was not so popular!'

Mrs Powell's recollections of the late 1920s in Colchester include: 'We used cut up newspaper to wipe our bottoms . . . Our next door neighbours were an elderly couple who cleaned the toilets in the nearby bus station. Their toilet was better than ours in my eyes as they had pieces of the magazine *John Bull* for their toilet paper and when I spent time with them I always asked to go to their lavatory, as we called it then, so I could piece together the pieces and read them – something I was not allowed to do at home!'

Less enthusiastically, Mr Wilson talks of the use of newspaper squares in Bradfield: 'It was usually quite a hunt for the continuance of the piece you had just finished reading, sometimes on standing up you could see the piece you wanted to read had already been used amongst the contents of the bucket. One night Mum was bathing me and she said, "Boy, whatever have you got on you?", while scrubbing the cheeks of my nether region, "Oh! I see, it's newsprint, it's coming off!"'

[6]

NOT SO PRIVATE . . .

The term 'privy' may have derived from the Latin word 'privatus', meaning apart or secret, but not everyone was alone on that journey down the garden path . . .

A common 'shared experience' was in the double privies often found behind rows of cottages. 'There were two separate doors but only one seat which covered the two buckets. We were told it was like being on a seesaw if both were in use at the same time.'

Judith Abbott remembers relations on the outskirts of Colchester who had flush toilets – with a difference: 'They did not have gardens, only yards, but they had an outside toilet just by the back door. The only problem was that this

Two privies for adjacent cottages at Coggeshall.

48

toilet was attached to your neighbour's property with no wall in between. The varnished toilet seat had two holes in it, one for you and one for your neighbour. There were no buckets just an open drain which ran away into a sewer . . . The only advantage was that if you ran out of paper you could "borrow" your neighbour's. It was a known thing that the two men of adjoining houses used to take their newspapers to read and have a smoke and a chat while in "residence".'

Mrs Shearing, now approaching her eightieth year, shares her memories with us: 'My parents, with five of us children, lived at Town End, Writtle, in one of Farmer Knowles's cottages at three shilling a week. The privy was joined onto next door's and one winter night I was sitting there and there was a very loud cough which came from the man next door sitting the other side. My word! I was so frightened I shot off screaming to Mum. When it was dark we carried a lighted candle in a 2lb jam jar with a string handle . . . on the roof I remember there was a cactus-like plant (house leek, or sempervivum) and we always called them "corns".'

Then there were the two and three (and sometimes more) holers. So many memories . . .

Miss Joslin was intrigued as a five-year-old in the early part of this century with the 'little house' in a cottage garden close to Little Graces near Little Baddow: 'It had a large wooden seat, with a big hole for adults and a small one for children. Even now I can imagine the horror of falling into the nasty depths below. I hated it.'

Mrs Moon of Weeley has a gem of a childhood privy memory: ' "Going down the bricks" was a phrase familiar in my early childhood when, having no indoor lavatory, we took the brick path to the little house at the bottom of the garden. A coat, umbrella and lantern hung inside the back door for cold, wet, dark nights.

'We lived for a time on a farm and the "little house" or privy

A two-holer at Park Farm, Great Waltham. Still in working order!

was quite palatial. It was just beyond the wash-house and boasted a three-holer mounted on a dais. Before school my sister and I would sit on the two smaller holes drumming our heels against the thunderboxes and singing lustily *Onward Christian Soldiers* or *Marching Through Georgia.* On the whitewashed walls hung a faded text: "The hearing ear, the seeing eye, the Lord hath made even both of them." If He ever regretted it, it was probably our fault.' Mrs Moon's experience then came in useful when she joined the ATS and was stationed in remote camps in Scotland and Belgium with far more primitive privies.

Hilda Collins remembers similar experiences at Little Leighs: 'When I was six years old and my sister ten we moved to Little Leighs Hall, then divided and shared with another family. To reach the toilet we had to go round the house and garden – through a gate at the back – turn right down a long path with a very high yew hedge on one side with a big open area of nut bushes on the other. At the bottom of the path the privy was situated over a stream that ran from the orchard down to the river. Inside was a bench with three different-sized holes to sit on. After heavy rain one sat over rushing water! As you can imagine going down there in the dark with a torch was very eerie.'

Mike Piper's grandparents ran the post office, general stores and the garage as well as a boarding house at Guyvers, Brewers End, Takeley, in the 1930s. They had a 'double' with two seats side by side, well away from the house, at the end of a row of outhouses. It was 'of tarred wood construction, approximately five feet by two feet six – it had no windows or artificial lighting so it was a dark, draughty, smelly hole . . . The cesspit into which everything dropped was under the building, extending out into the garden where it had a wooden cover.

'It was a ritual when we wanted to go to the lavvy as we were always accompanied by an adult. At night we carried a little oil lamp which usually blew out on the way and had to be relit when we were inside. I remember how ghostly and eerie it was and how the adult would keep saying, "Hurry up! It's freezing!" If I can recall correctly my grandparents always used to go up together in the morning and my grandad always smoked his pipe. Whether the boarders went in two by two I cannot say. I have vivid memories of Nurse Shaw, the District Nurse, who was a boarder; she was a very, very large lady and must have completely filled the tiny space.

'As to the upkeep, Ethel Rolph, the general maid, had the privilege of scrubbing the wooden seat every day and pouring disinfectant into the pit. Henry Spiller emptied it, using a long-handled scoop and a wooden wheelbarrow, and emptied the contents into a hole at the bottom which was then covered with earth. One could smell the odour for days after – but it grew lovely rhubarb.'

Elwin Hurst recalls his father taking on the tenancy of the farm at Rochford Hall in the 1930s and clearly remembers

'. . . a little one for children . . .' The farmhouse privy at Rochford Hall.

the old brick-built privy with its sloping, tiled roof which still had the earth closets from much earlier times. 'Along the back wall, as you entered, was one of about eight feet in length with two holes, each with a fitting lid, and in the corner behind the door was a little one for children – a square box with a hole and a lid.

'There was no lighting and so on a winter evening I can remember sitting there with father for company, an oil light or lantern flickering, wondering why there were two holes for the grown-ups? With the wisdom of time I expect it was an expedient measure to "spread" the excrement and so extend the periods between emptying. The privy was there, and in good condition, when my parents left Rochford Hall for a smaller house in 1973 . . .'

An industrial anecdote is recounted by John Jay: 'I was apprenticed to Crompton Parkinson Ltd in Chelmsford from 1944. By that time there were proper indoor toilet facilities. There were, however, stories still circulating of an earlier period when the workers' toilets were in an outside building which consisted of a number of cubicles built over a trough with running water flowing along under the row of seats. It was said that one of the apprentices' tricks was to wait until the seats were occupied and set fire to a crumpled ball of newspaper which could then be floated down the trough while still alight! Were the sitters' cheeks red?'

A six-seater – no less – is described by Mrs Page who was brought up on Hill Farm, North Stifford. This one had to cater for the convenience of farmhands and family alike. It was a small brick building with a chimney pot on the top and the seating was arranged 'back to back, for women and girls on one side, men and boys on the other. I didn't like friends having to use it. During the war bombs were dropped, aimed at the nearby gun site. The blast damaged our privy so my brothers put a notice on it which stated:

BOMBED OUT AND BLASTED
BUT BUSINESS GOES ON
AS USUAL

This caused many a laugh!'

Mrs D. Ritchie from Navestock Side, Brentwood, gives a charming, child's-eye view of sanitation at home and school: 'As a small child I lived in the school house attached to the village school in Rettendon where my father was headmaster from 1924–28 and I have a clear memory of our "privy".

'On leaving the back door of the house you had to cross the "Back Yard". Along the righthand side were the back windows of classrooms, on the left was the way down our large garden divided by a long and very abundant archway of roses. It gave protection from the rain on your way to the privy, which was part of a large brick building known as the Wash House. You went up a high step into the privy which had whitewashed walls and a stone floor, and there were gaps at the top and bottom of the door which let in cold winds, rain and snow!

'As we were so young my sister and I never had to make the journey through the rose arch after dark. Adults used to take an oil lamp with them and I thought it looked very spooky, especially on windy nights. We were allowed to use a chamber pot in the bedroom through the winter evenings and this was emptied into a "slop pail" made of enamel, with a lid, which was carried to the privy in the morning.

'There was an old man (as he appeared to a little girl) named Mr Snell, odd-job man and gardener at the school, who came round twice a day with a wooden yoke across his shoulders with chains dangling from it. To them he attached the handles of the buckets in the privies and carried them to a distant spot at the far end of the garden where there was a cesspit – out of bounds to us. Needless to say my sister and I christened the poor man Mr **Smell**!'

Talking of schools . . . an anonymous contributor – I wonder if he was the guilty party – tells of a young lad who didn't like a fellow pupil, a little girl, at the village school in Stisted. 'When he saw her go into the privy he got a bunch of stinging nettles, opened the flap at the back and pushed them in. They never found the culprit!'

A marvellous Doulton chamber pot, shown outside the old privy at Ebenezer Cottage, Boreham.

[7]

JUST GOING DOWN THE GARDEN

Mrs Lillian Lambert of West Mersea has written a most evocative account of her privy life: '252 steps! The times I counted these . . . it felt such a long way "down the garden" when you were in desperate need of the toilet.

'From five years of age I grew up with the "lav", or "dyke" as we called it, until I was fifteen years old. We lived in East Street, Tollesbury, on the site of a fifteenth century pub, now occupied by an extension to Tollesbury school.

'The summer was no easier than winter months for me to make my visits. During these late summer months two dreadful events happened: the first was spiders – long, leggy harvest ones. These hung from every possible wooden surface in huge clusters. I used to swing the black, tar-painted, wooden door back gingerly, then slam it back hard, and wait for the spiders to scuttle across the floor to the garden. Then I would rush across the lino covered floor to sit on what I hoped was a spider-free seat.

'At the back of the dyke shed wall was a flap, on hinges, for access to the buckets from outside when they needed emptying. The second dreaded summer event was the "bucket man". He always arrived earlier than in the winter, and I dreaded getting caught, in the early morning, before school, still performing! I sang so many songs, for I'd been told that "men whistle and ladies sing" to let folk know that the place was occupied. From "Incy, Wincy Spider" to the Beatles – I sang loudly. The "bucket man" only caught me out once! I hid up in the corner very quietly whilst he emptied and replaced the bucket. The contents were taken to a village cesspit down Woodrope. Newspapers were torn, as you sat down, into squares ready for the next person.

Which privy should receive the accolade for picturesqueness? It must be this peaceful retreat, viewed front and back, in Boreham. (Photograph courtesy of Derek Bircher)

'One year the *Daily Sketch* published a photo of a cloud forming an image of Jesus. I thought it would be awful to "use" Jesus, so I carefully tore out the picture, folded it and hit it up in a corner of a wooden joist.

'When the snow came I followed bird and animal tracks

Timothy the cat, held by Joan Harrington, within sight of Lillian Lambert's old privy at Tollesbury.

and tried to step in my own prints en route to the communal tap in the garden to wash my hands. It rarely froze because it was warmly lagged with sacking. The contents of the bucket **did** freeze over – not a pleasant sight! Darkness was scary! The cycle torch was the best one to use. It was easy to stand it down on the seat or hang from a hook on the door. Shadow pictures formed in its light – hedgehogs and other creatures snuffled around outside. Owls hooted – hurry up! . . . scratching began! It was my cat – he usually followed me along the path and waited outside but in the winter he would scratch the door to come in with me. There **was** a dyke closer to our house than the one we used: I have just learned, from my mother, that we swapped toilets with an elderly neighbour, because she could no longer walk to hers.

'When I was fourteen my friend's parents, over the road, allowed me to use their indoor toilet. What luxury! I held on until I could go over there morning and evening! Doesn't that sound incredible? It seems impossible that we were so primitive only those few years ago. My age? I am 49. I didn't think I was living history – but there you are!'

Marjorie Griggs of Ickleton, near Saffron Walden, is 89 years old. She remembers well the 'little house' at the bottom of the garden. She married in 1931 and when she came here the "loo" was a long way from the back door. At first it was over a cesspit which had to be emptied from the back by one of our farm labourers, then we got pails. We had to have two seats, one with a step for the children to get on. It was a long way to go on a winter's night. When my sister used to visit me and wanted to go to the loo she would say, "I will have to go up Six Mile Bottom!" There is a village with that name, near Newmarket."

Mrs Edwards of Brentwood gives a sharply drawn picture of sanitary provision 'at our old cottage in Coxtie Green. The path to it measured approximately 27–30 feet. On opening the back door of the kitchen after a night's snowfall we would be confronted by a wall of snow which had drifted halfway up the door. Out came the shovels quickly to clear the way, but wellingtons or tall boots were a must to negotiate the deep snow on the path. By the time we had sufficiently cleared the path using pans of hot water we couldn't reach the privy quickly enough!'

Norman Croft of Brentwood remembers: 'My mother had numerous relatives in Great Bardfield. As a schoolboy in the late 1920s and throughout the 1930s I frequently visited one of them in a 17th century, thatched cottage. Main sewage disposal and electricity were not available until after the Second World War, so the sanitary arrangements were provided by a privy at the end of a one-hundred-foot-long garden, approached by a muddy path. The privy consisted of a pit that was some six feet deep with the sides riveted with timber planks. The pit top was traversed by timber beams which supported a timber shack with a floor which was about four feet square. Seating arrangements consisted of a plank platform with a rough sawn single-holer provided, all surfaces worn splinter-free by the posteriors of previous users. The constructor of this device did not anticipate the employment of a gongfermer to undertake the periodic removal of the contents of the pit, for no access facility was provided. Probably he assumed that the soak away pit base, and microbic action, would keep the contents from building up and requiring removal, although it did seem to me that the danger level was approached at times. The privy was built at the turn of the century or earlier. Over the years masses of ivy had overgrown the structure so that none of the timber,

Then and now in Great Bardfield . . . A weatherboarded hut replaced in 1941 by a modern flush toilet, both outside.

apart from the door was visible. From the outside it looked like a gigantic long-tailed tit's nest!

'Toilet paper was provided by the pages of the *News of the World* which was apparently my relative's sole source of news and titillation. The sheets were large squares (four per page). This allowed users of the privy (presumably suffering from defective olfactory nerves) to sit and enjoy complete articles. My main memory of the privy is of the awful stench. I would postpone a visit as long as I could, then take a deep breath, hold it, and make a dash for it. I had to tread carefully inside because I had a horror of the rotten, creaking floor giving way and landing me literally in the dirt! The time would come when I could hold my breath no longer and gasped in the air of that stomach-churning effluvia.

'Early in the war my mother left her London home and rented a cottage close to her uncle's. It had a sentry-box-like privy, thirty feet down the garden. It had a lift-up flap at the rear which enabled a large bucket, sited under the loo seat, to be removed for emptying and cleaning. Such cleaning every day, and the liberal application of pink lavatory powder gave an odourless and quite acceptable form of sanitation. But there were rats in the garden and I was afraid of getting a bite on my bottom after dark, so before entering it I would walk around the sentry box kicking the sides and would then shine a powerful torch inside the bucket housing. Despite its lack of odour the sentry box was not in use for long, being replaced by a flush toilet attached to the house and discharging into a cesspit.

'In the 1950s the village was connected to main drainage.'

'It was a dark and cold winter's night,' so starts the atmospheric tale from John Young of Hornchurch, 'hoar frost hung from the trees as the cottages in our village huddled together under their thatched roofs in an effort to keep out the cold. To an outsider only an occasional flicker from a candle or paraffin lamp through an uncurtained window betrayed the existence of human life.

'Inside our cottage Father rested in his rocking chair

reading the newspaper. Mother had been at the washtub all day and my brother and I were playing on the floor with our Meccano set. We had constructed a miniature threshing machine and were busy pretending to be threshing corn from the ricks built in the Manor Farm rickyard, charging Father a halfpenny a rick threshed and he was paying in buttons from Mother's button box as she sat darning and sewing at the table.

'Suddenly I had the call – very urgently. "Mum," I yelled, as I backed out from under the table, "I want to go to the privy!" Like all good privies ours was at the end of the garden, twenty yards away. I suppose ours was a rather grand affair, having a double throne – in other words the wooden seat had two holes, one for adults and a smaller one for children, each covered with a loose wooden lid. It gave a comfy feeling to be able to sit side by side doing what comes naturally. In a recess on one wall was a pile of squares of newspaper and on a shelf at the other end Father kept his tools. A privet hedge shielded the door from prying eyes. At the side of the privy, covered by a sheet of corrugated iron, was the cesspit which had to be emptied about twice a year. This was an occasion the whole village knew about because we had to help dig a big hole in the garden and, after dark, Father had to empty the cesspit bucket by bucket and then cover it all over.

'"Be quick," said Mother. "Put your coat on and take the candle and Bill will go with you." Bill was older than me, supposedly frightened of nothing; but rats lurked at the bottom of the garden on such nights as this; "Oh, Mum," he said, but she replied, "There's nothing to be frightened of." I had already got my coat on and was holding the candle. "Come on, Bill, be quick!" I shouted, hopping from one leg to the other, and together we dashed up the garden. I pushed open the privy door and dumped the candle on the shelf, Bill whipped off the lid and I hauled down my trousers and sank thankfully back on the privy.

63

'"You'll be alright now," said Bill, in a hurry to get back to the threshing. "No-o-o, wait for me!" I cried, fearful of the dark and shivering with cold. Something scampered past the door in the candle's flickering light. "What was that?"

'"A rat I expect," answered Bill, trying to sound brave. At last the job was done. Bill grabbed the candle and with my trousers somewhere round my knees we made a dash back down the garden and into the warmth and light and safety of home. "Alright?" queries Mother. "Nothing to be frightened of was there?"

'"Y-y-yes," I started to blurt out, but Bill gave me a sharp dig in the ribs – there was more threshing to be done before bedtime!'

[8]

CESSPITS AND SCOOPS

Of course, as we have heard, someone had to empty the bucket or scoop out the pit and I think we should spare a thought for the heroes who carried out this task.

Jack Shelley, who was born in Galleywood, one of eleven children, in the early part of this century, remembers: 'There was plenty of activity in the "lavvy" or "bumby" as they were generally known. Being one of the oldest boys in the family I was very often called upon to "Empty the Bumby". The structure of our "lavvy" was of a frame building some 6 ft wide by 4 ft deep with a tiled roof and a tarred weatherboard cladding. The back had a sloping lid or flap which allowed the two buckets to be withdrawn rearwards. Other kinds had a brick-lined pit from which the contents had to be shovelled out into a wheelbarrow for burial in a trench in the garden.

'We had one of each type because the original cottage had another one built onto it. The newer one, which I emptied, had two seats, to accommodate adults and children. The other one was cleared by a neighbour and his son-in-law who grew vegetables to sell locally. They would come with their large wheelbarrow, one holding the handles and the other had a rope tied to the front of the barrow which he put over his shoulder to tow with . . . that's how I first experienced "recycling" for we were regularly sent round to them for beautiful vegetables!

'The sewers did not come to Galleywood until after World War II so when we moved up to newly built council houses in 1925 we still had the old system.'

Judith Abbott has never forgotten visits to her aunt when the privy was still doing very good business, as we might say: '. . . buckets needed emptying more often and Dad offered to do the "dirty deed". The toilet was a corrugated tin shed alongside a cow field (flies were a problem) with a step up into it. The buckets were placed under a "bench" seat which had two holes in it to suit large and small bottoms. My Dad lifted up the bucket by its handle with two hands, it was quite heavy as you can imagine, and promptly slipped on the step covering himself with the contents!'

Judith's other aunt and uncle lived at the bottom of the village in a row of council houses. Digging the hole for the emptying of the bucket had to be a clandestine affair, done in the dark according to the etiquette of the time. In Act Two of the performance we see Judith's aunt buying her 'chitterlings' – pig's intestines, popular then as a cheap food when money was short. She put them to soak in a bucket. Meanwhile Uncle had dug the hole, came back, picked up the bucket and buried – the chitterlings! When Auntie realised the situation she went out and helped to dig them up and rinse them off, while Uncle attended to that **other** bucket! Next morning the neighbours asked what was all that commotion in the garden last night?

Mrs Wright's story reflects the true spirit of wartime Britain: 'On a night in 1940 my husband embarked for North Africa to fight the Germans. The same night a German pilot flew over London and dropped a bomb on our brand new home. My husband's ship was torpedoed that same night and he was landed with other survivors in Scotland. With self-preservation in mind I decided to return to my mother's roots in Layer-de-la-Haye. A relative found us a rented house and five of us moved in. Certain amenities were pointed out – one: a water pump **inside** the kitchen complete with fitted sink which regularly flooded, and two: a covered extension from the back door to the privy, in the shape of a tin roof, some planks of wood and two broken windows. I enquired what arrangements were made to "service" the privy, my relative looked surprised and said: "I have dug a trench at the bottom of the garden. Fill it in as you go along." My sister and I finally realised it was up to us. I still had a precious bottle of prewar lavender water. I went upstairs, put a liberal sprinkling of the perfume onto a large handkerchief which I tied round my face – and played my part in the War Effort! We were still digging trenches at the bottom of the garden when my husband came home five years later!'

Dick Wilkins gives a graphic description of Eastwood before the war: 'Where people had no garden to bury their waste products a man would call to collect their buckets and empty them into a two-wheeled tumbril cart, pulled by a horse. In terraces without a back alley it was necessary for the "lavender man" as he was called to carry the bucket from the privy right through the front room and out of the front door; of course, occasionally some of the stinking liquid spilt on the floor. The stink from the "lavender cart" could carry a quarter of a mile down wind.'

Patrick Rea-Allison of Benfleet reports on his privy days: 'For a period of our married life during the war we had to find lodgings to keep together. One of these was a group of terraced houses. In the middle of the terrace was an arched passage to give access to the dustmen for the bins and the privy men for the buckets. I was a particularly light sleeper – unfortunately the privies were always emptied between two and three in the morning – and by a **one-armed man**! This man had a hook for his hand, which he used to carry the bucket, swinging and banging against the wall of that passageway . . . I am now over 78 years old and I still think at times during the night I can hear that bucket going Bang, Bang, BANG!!!'

A brand new but authentic privy bucket, nostalgically adorned by Judith Abbott with the 'Roses and Castles' design once practised by bargees on the canals.

High Easter Memorial School privies.

Derek Bircher's memories of privies in High Easter are comprehensive and illuminating: 'When I arrived in the village as a boy in 1934, most of the houses and the two schools had the wooden-seat-with-bucket-under sanitation. The buckets of the Chapel School were attended to by a man called Joe Little who was then a council roadman. He had a large area of his garden not far from the school where he had his "bumby" – most cottages at this time had their own bumby hole in their gardens. Joe's job of seeing to the school buckets was not part of his council employment, so it would have given him a little extra income. When needed he would take the buckets and empty them into his bumby hole and cover the deposit with earth.

'Since no Night Cart or Soil Cart service was provided by the council another service Joe offered was a weekly soil barrow collection in the village. For this he used a large wooden wheelbarrow in which he put a quantity of wood or coal ash. Generally on Friday afternoons he could be seen pushing his barrow up the Cock Lane which ran up behind the village street. His charge for each bucket emptied was 6d. It was a necessary service for widows, maiden ladies and those with small gardens.

'Of course, not all the privies were fitted with buckets, some used a system where there was a large pit beneath the seat. At intervals this pit had to be emptied by men using long-handled scoops. A few houses had an Elsan chemical lavatory, but, with few exceptions, this needed to be emptied, although the company did produce one model which had a very large tank under, and a soak-away system which needed no further attention once installed. Some privies were fitted with a dry earth or ash box, where a quantity of earth or ash was released after use, but these were not very general in High Easter.'

Hilda Rust, 82, of Shalford remembers: 'I lived in a row of five cottages on the road to Wethersfield. Four of us kids and Mum. Privy up the hill at the back – a two-seater, scrubbed every week with Monday's washing water. We sat over a large pit dug under a combined pair of privies, emptied when needed by my two brothers with a fet – a scoop on a long handle – into buckets – onto our garden. Later collected in a "bushel" or tanker lorry laid on by the Lord of the Manor. We kids called it the Marmalade Cart much to Mum's disgust for she thought it was wonderful.'

From Canvey Island Mr Bickford tells a story which well illustrates the period between private privy and public toilet. 'In the summer of 1947 I went to work for C.W. Goulding's sheetmetal factory in Canvey Point Road. The Elsan toilet for the workers was located round the back in a U-shaped inlet between one old barn and two Nissen huts. To get the "toilet" emptied the foreman had to persuade one of the lads to do it, mainly by offering fifteen minutes overtime or, in desperation, thirty minutes. As the Elsan was nearly always overflowing we needed quite some persuading!'

Mr Werner of Brentwood describes three different sorts of emptying: 'The first time I came into contact with a privy was when I was courting my wife over fifty years ago. We lived on Laindon Common, Billericay, I was lodging at her parents' house at the time. The "privy" was a wooden structure, a short distance from the house. One had to sit on wooden boards, underneath was a large hole with an opening at the back (a cesspit), when full the contents were shovelled out with a long-handled contraption into a bucket which was then emptied into the vegetable garden, especially into the rows of potatoes.

'My second experience was when my wife and I were living at Lapwater Hall near Brentwood, once a farm, but after a bomb was dropped on it during the war, all that remained was the air raid shelter. We had a caravan on the site and used the shelter as a lavatory. All we had in it was an old "Elsan" bucket which, every so often, I had to empty into a hole which I had dug beforehand.

'My third experience was when we moved to Childerditch, Brentwood. The lavatory was outside, next to the old bake-house. Our neighbour at the time informed us on our first day, about all the people who would call weekly with food, oil, coke, etc. He also mentioned that every Tuesday the "Penny Man" came at 7 am to empty our bucket. I could not believe that someone had such a job and my wife and I thought our neighbour was having a joke with us. But on the next Tuesday, right on 7 am, I looked out of the window and, sure enough, there was the Penny Man carrying our bucket to his lorry, emptying it and returning to our outside privy! He was dressed in overalls, wearing large gloves. We always gave him a large "Christmas Box" – we thought he deserved it.'

Mrs Edwards describes a more 'high tech' collection from her privy in Coxtie Green: 'A cesspool was situated beside it which the Council would empty twice a year via special pipes attached to a large container which was stationed on the road outside. These were carried and fixed together through our sideway. Whilst it was in operation the large pipes used to vibrate owing to the throb of the suction engine, and I shall never forget on one occasion, our cat standing a few feet away watching the pipes and hearing the noise, its hair on end, ears back, eyes bulging, and gradually backing away, wondering what sort of animal or snake it was looking at!'

I am reminded of the unfortunate experience of one intrepid collector of buckets. He and his mate had started

'Lavender men' at work, pictured by Jim Foster.

72

out so early that a coat was needed. But he was getting hotter and hotter carrying those buckets on a yoke across his shoulders. He took off his coat and hitched it on the cart.

A couple of hours later they paused for a rest and a bite to eat. He reached up for his coat to get his sandwiches – and found it wasn't there! Just one sleeve poking up from the collected sewage signalled its fate. He hauled it out, and gave a shout of delight. 'It's alright, my sandwiches are safe!' We must remember that in those days there was no such thing as waterproof wrapping and plastic bags. . .

[9]

HORROR STORIES

Mrs Wilson of Witham remembers her grandmother's privy with nostalgia tinged with disgust – 'Ugh! How it smelt; I wouldn't use it' – and her aunt's privy just a few yards away is remembered for its nettles: 'Not only was it a revolting experience to use, but big, ugly stinging nettles grew in profusion around the door, out of every crack in the cement of the path. We often got our bare legs stung unless we were very careful!'

═══════════════

Rats jumped out of my postbag from all corners of the county when I was researching this book. 'My father normally emptied the bucket,' Monty Seabrook of Gosfield told me, 'but when he was unwell it was my job, or sometimes my mother had to step in. Often at night when I went I would hear a rat scuttle away, for we had rats in our roof spaces because our houses were converted from oxen sheds with thatched roofs.' 'When we had a cat', Mrs Wilson of Clavering shuddered, 'and you had to use the privy on a rough and windy night you could be sure of having to step over a dead rat just outside the door!' And it wasn't just rats that caused the terror, as Mrs Chipperfield of Goldhanger explained, 'When I first married our privy was at least fifty yards up the garden – behind it was a deep ditch where you could hear the rats squelching and squeaking. Not a place to go on one's own after dark! I remember one dark, wet night, hundreds of worms had come out of the wet grass onto the path. When the torchlight fell on them they slid back with great speed into the grass. I was so petrified by these pink, slimy things appearing and disappearing that my husband, who had walked up the garden with me, had to carry me back to the house. After that it was some time before I was brave enough to venture up the garden at night!'

More seriously, there was this sad report in the *Essex Standard* of 1852:

On 1st April the Rev. Henry G.N. Bishop saw in the water closet in his garden, and under the closet immediately adjoining, used by the servants, the mutilated remains of a child, and these were subsequently examined by Dr. Edward Webb Dowman of Clacton . . . Helen Venus alias White appeared before the magistrates at the Maids Head Inn, Thorpe, on 12th April, and was committed to the Assizes. She was a servant recently employed by the vicar, and the child was hers.

All the evidence against the poor unfortunate girl is repeated. There was, no doubt, a good deal of sympathy, but justice must be seen to have been done. Helen was convicted only of concealing the birth of a child and for that she served twelve months in prison with hard labour.

Mr H. Osborne had experience as a boy of using an earth closet: 'It consisted of the seat and bucket, but behind your back was a wooden box that was filled with peat moss and had a lever-type handle which, when pulled, deposited a measured amount into the bucket to cover the excrement.' He also illustrates the disadvantage of the privy sited well down the garden when one of his elderly relatives had an urgent call of nature late one night. Off he dashed – flung open the door, and in the moonlight saw a tramp asleep on the seat. The shock could have caused a nasty accident!

Mr Woodgate of Colchester was brought up in a cottage in the country with a two-mile walk to a spring for their water supply; '. . . our lavvy was at the bottom of our garden – a small shed – and when the bucket was full we took it in turns to empty it in the garden. First we had to dig a deep hole – if it wasn't deep enough you know what happened! But I must say my father grew rhubarb with stems like walking sticks.

'When my sister went to the toilet once something cold touched her backside. After screaming she looked down and what did she see in the bucket? – the ferret we had lost months ago which we thought had gone for good!'

Dorothy Rowlinson's husband had a memorable encounter as a boy: '. . . on a pitch black night he took the usual walk. As he sat upon the seat he put his hand down on a damp furry object. He nearly took off through the roof with fright. He went back into the house to get a light to identify what felt like a dead cat. Not so! Someone had left behind a fur glove! After that he got himself his own torch!'

I'll let Dick Wilkins sum up: 'In summer there were the added inconveniences of spiders, ants, wasps and, now and again, a mouse or a bat. These coupled with the consumption of rhubarb and apple jam made, you might say, from the fruit of our labours, saw to it that none of our family ever needed any other laxative.'

[10]

ONE HAD TO LAUGH

Modern toilets are hygienic, clinical, so clean and bright with gleaming paintwork and germproof plastic seats, so handy within the house or flat; but they cannot equal the old garden privy in the anecdotes and almost loving memories which are recounted by the senior 'sitters' of Essex.

Tony Jay lived in Albert Street, Colchester, from 1945 to 1970; '. . . my mother continued to live there until her death in 1995, and all this time we had to go down the garden, a short one, to use it. As boys, my brother and I would sit on the throne and throw our pen knives into the wooden door about eighteen inches in front of us; a bounce back could have cut us off in our prime! For a laugh we would loop cotton onto the inside bolt, pass it out over the top of the door and pull it from the outside, thus locking it. Many a time my Dad had to undo the external "T" hingers to get the door open again, followed, I might add, by his hand round an ear or his belt across a tender area.

'On one occasion a neighbour was seen by us boys trying to make good speed up her garden path with her knickers round her ankles, and screaming very loudly. The reason? – a rat sitting by the outlet pipe at the back of the privy seat! Another incident was at a party on a very, very cold Boxing Day in the 'sixties. One young man got extremely drunk and spent the night clinging to the privy seat, sprawled out through the open door, simply repeating to one and all, "Don't touch me!" The other lads at the party used the ditch behind it – but the ladies were cross-legged! When he was coaxed away at 4 am the miscreant was covered in snow and ice.

'In later years after I had left home my parents still used

Nature has become a squatter in this privy at East Hanningfield.

the "outside bog", as it was affectionately known. When they got older the council installed an indoor loo as part of a "stay put" scheme, but my Mum still used the outsider most of the time, at least till bedtime . . .'

Mrs Spendley passes on her 89-year-old Mum's memory of the privy at West Street, Harwich. When she was a young girl she booked her place in the privy each week when the choir was rehearsing hymns for Sunday in the chapel next door – she can still sing those hymns, though she had never seen them in a hymn book.

Mrs Bueggeln's grandparents had a farm on the borders of Rainham and Upminster with two privies side by side – a single and a double. 'One had a broken floor and I was terrified of falling through to the cesspit below. This fear stayed with me always. My uncles used to play tricks on the lodger by putting a guy on the seat at night to frighten him when he came home drunk.' The farm was burned down in 1965 and the remains were bulldozed – two more privies lost to history.

A touching anonymous letter reminds us of hard times during the Battle of Britain: '. . . our family left home to stay with relatives in Essex leaving my father still in London. After a few months we decided to make the move permanent, so my father left London with the removal van to join us. It was a stroke of luck because next morning our house was bombed. At the bottom of the garden of our rented house was the privy. It was a bit frightening to go down there at night with a torch and suddenly to have a frog jump on your foot! The "night-soil men" used to call once a week with a sort of tank to empty the buckets, usually at dusk. I was in there one night when I heard them coming down the garden so I got out quickly and hid round the other side until they'd gone.'

Mr Garwood of Danbury recalls the privy of his young days: '. . . sitting on this toilet with the door open watching searchlights pick out a German bomber which was shot down by a night fighter. It crashed in Springfield Road, Chelmsford, in the garden of the Bishop of that diocese.'

Patrick Rea-Allison tells a story of when he was a commercial traveller in Essex. 'One of my calls was a small country shop between Brentwood and Doddinghurst, owned by a dear old lady. One day I went in the shop and found no-one about. I thought this was strange so I went right through to the back garden and called her name. There was a faint reply from what appeared to be a pile of shedding and corrugated iron. On moving much of this I discovered my dear old lady sitting on the privy still with her knickers round her legs and in a very distressed state. Apparently the whole privy just fell in on her as she was sitting there. She later presented me with a pair of gold cuff links which I wear and treasure still today.'

Mrs Ida Cunningham tells a nice story about her days at the old Manor Farm, Great Baddow, from 1928: '. . . the old privy was a real relic. In the bad weather it was no joke as we had to cross the farmyard to reach it . . . my brothers made a lantern to use at night. It was an old biscuit tin with glass windows and a piece of candle inside. Coming up to Christmas the big farmyard was full of turkeys being fattened up for market. With the old "stag" or turkeycock on guard it was difficult to get across to the loo. We had an old aunt visiting; we children didn't like her because she was too bossy. She was afraid of nothing – until she had to do battle with the stag. She had a call of nature – off she went, armed with a walking stick and ready for the fray. She had only gone a couple of yards when she came face to face with her enemy. She hit out with her stick until she dropped it, then kicked out with her foot until she lost her slipper. We youngsters stood around – it was the best laugh of the week – my older brothers got a telling off from Mum, but I think that she, too, must have had a little chuckle. Anyway, Auntie went back to

Sunderland the next day and we never saw or heard from her again.'

Janet Woods' story of her grandparents' privy out at Wickham Bishops is a classic example of tact – or temerity! As recently as the 1980s 'my grandparents lived in a farm cottage with no hot water and only an outside privy. This was brick-built and joined to the house, which was very lonely and, when I was young, surrounded by an orchard. You can imagine that, as children, their granddaughters, not liking the dark, used to go in convoy with a torch and all crowd in together. My grandfather was using it one evening, reading the daily paper as he usually did, with the door open, as they did not have the luxury of a light. On hearing footsteps he looked up to see a lady walk past. She immediately turned back and said to my grandfather that she was looking for his letterbox. My grandfather replied that they didn't have one. The lady took a step towards the privy and handed my grandfather some pamphlets, saying she would leave them with him and went on her way.

'The pamphlets were for the Labour Party – the local elections were due. When the local candidate visited to canvas for votes my grandfather said that one his ladies had been recently. The candidate said, with a smile, that he had heard of the visit.'

One last anecdote was sworn as faithfully true when recounted by an old shipmate recently. We first met on a minesweeper when we were clearing the Mediterranean of mines in 1945–6. Jack was always complaining of the terrible conditions in which his widowed mother lived in a cottage out in the Dengie peninsular. He was fed up with all the promises from the politicians of 'homes for heroes to live in'. He said he'd do something about it when he was demobbed. He knew that you couldn't live in a house without a toilet, and his mother had to use a privy way up the garden, and empty it herself, and that just wasn't good enough. When we returned to the UK he took with him just one hand-grenade from the store we kept to explode a certain kind of mine.

When we met up again he told me the end of the drama. It was a moonlit night as he crept round the cottage and saw the privy standing four-square in the moonlight. He got near enough take a throw and wreck the wretched hut. The grenade went off with such a bang; the blast blew out the sides of the privy, and there in the moonlight sat his mother, with her knickers about her ankles, safe, but shocked. 'Oh! Mum!' he said, 'I'm that sorry.'

'Tha's orlroight bhoy,' she said, 'tha' mus' ha' bin sumthin' Oi et!'

[11]

SOME OF THE SURVIVORS

Privies, in my time, and in my experience of their use, were always cleanly-kept places, almost dignified in the way in which they cloaked their prime purpose – and managed to look like garden sheds! We have visited many of those which survive in Essex. Which should get first mention? It has to be the only privy in Essex listed by the Department of the Environment as worthy of preservation, forming part of the interesting old house at Foxton's Farm, Ugley Green, no more than twenty yards up the garden path.

When Mrs Doggett was a child in this, her parents' house, a light was always shining from a window to show her the way to and from the privy – a guiding star. The wooden seat is original and the bucket is an honoured relic of days of constant use. Knotholes in the weatherboarding show the age of the timbers. The roof tiles are original and there is no doubt that this privy had a century of use before it was finally outmoded by the main drainage which crept out into rural Essex in the first half of the 20th century.

Park Farm, Great Waltham, is the home of Jill Cowley, the well-known expert on gardening. In the days when the privy in her own glorious garden was in constant use by a farmer and his family it was taken for granted as a very necessary building. Today it is surrounded by flowers and trees and shrubs in decorative retirement, yet just as well maintained as a reminder of those Essex families who lived on this land, grew their food on it, and when their days were ended were buried in the land of the parish churchyard. Jill appreciates the significance of this obsolete little building and keeps it in good repair. She has even placed in that privy cut-up pieces of newspaper of the right size – and of the right date – by

The only listed privy in the county – carefully preserved at Foxton's Farm, Ugley Green.

Mrs Doggett's childhood privy. Note the deal seat with the front-opening door below, allowing easy removal of the bucket.

The privy at Park Farm, Great Waltham, stands under a walnut tree amid a wonderful garden.

using photocopies of an original newspaper which she cut to the correct size. We know that the privy is more than one hundred and twenty years old because it is actually marked, as an identifiable, small black square, on the Ordnance Survey map of Essex published in 1875.

It was due to the interest of Alan Weedon that we were able to look at a wonderful old privy – practically hidden behind a thick curtain of natural summer greenery – in Hempstead, in the interval between the death of its elderly owner and its adoption by a new generation. This was a real beauty! Behind the conglomeration of gardening gear we were just able to get a view of the Elsan pan, minus the seat, which would have been flushed with a bucket of water down into a cesspit beneath or adjacent. Proof of this was found in one implement still leaning against the wall after its last use many years ago. It is the 'fet' or scoop used to empty the cesspit when the sewage cart came round. On the other hand, the sewage may have been carried out into the extensive gardens for use as a natural fertiliser.

What a morning of pastoral privy pleasure we enjoyed with Mr and Mrs Bunting at Rye Farm, Layer-de-la-Haye! On a summer morning, deep in the Essex countryside we came to a farm on a hillock surrounded by water – an ancient moated site and a farmhouse of great historical and architectural significance with two very old and quite separate privies. One, it seems, would have been for the farmer and his family and the other for the farmhands then employed in much larger numbers. They both stand on the edge of the moat at either side of the farmhouse, but at some distance. The one nearest to the house, for the farmer himself, is on the very edge of the moat, completely festooned in ivy with its door jammed ajar by its intrusive growth. It was built in brick, with a window above the door to allow light and ventilation. In its day it was smartly painted white. No vestige of its interior furniture – bench or bucket – remains. In fact, from its

87

Alan Weedon with the 'fet' belonging to an old privy in Hempstead.

The farmhouse privy at Rye Farm.

position right on the moat it is most likely that it never had a bucket – the contents of the pit were drained, or were flushed with a bucket of water, straight into the moat – to the delight of fish and fowl.

Diametrically opposite on the 'island' stood the farmhands' privy, a standard lean-to against a brick barn. Its wooden construction has at some time been partly repaired with corrugated iron. Now it has been almost overgrown with cereal weeds, trees and the ubiquitous ivy. But the door stands edged open and within we found the wooden seat with the hole in the middle which must have seen many a bottom. Behind the rear, wooden wall we spotted a very unusual feature – a rusting piece of corrugated iron covering a wide shallow ditch which sloped away to the edge of moat. This was the chute which, with the aid of a bucket of water, took the sitter's excrement straightway down into the moat. This is the only occasion on which we found such a feature still in position, overgrown and corroded as it is.

Seen at Rye Farm: the rusting cover of the chute taking the privy contents down into the moat.

An example of the way in which an old privy has been taken over by a new owner and eventually modernised is provided by Eve Crawford and her neighbour at Coggeshall, the small town uniting the villages of Great and Little Coggeshall. Their adjoining cottages, within an ancient timber framework, have been tastefully modernised within and without. So have their privies, built as an adjoining pair at the end of the garden. The neighbour's has been converted into a shed without affecting the appearance of the exterior, but Eve's, changed to a flush toilet after her arrival there in 1958, still serves as a very useful back-up to the indoor, upstairs loo when the grandchildren descend en masse!

A standard type of Essex privy still exists as a feature of a house at Hatfield Broad Oak. When the present owners moved there they found a reminder of the problems of people who actually had to use the privy – a 'Flit' spray! They have preserved the privy, complete with seat and bucket,

A double privy, preserved at Hatfield Broad Oak. The bucket looks suspiciously like a 'slop pail' from the days when chamber pots were emptied in the house and the contents carried – under a discreet lid – to the privy for disposal.

which now looks over a swimming pool – testament of the great strides made in water supply and sanitation through this century.

And finally . . . It is amazing to find an outside privy still standing in the garden of a house right by the busy main road of Warley Hill and very close to the centre of Brentwood. Detached, brick-built, with a corrugated iron roof and now covered in creepers, it dates from about 1860. It was refitted in the 20th century with a modern flush 'loo' but Rod and Mary Beaumont now house part of their collection of secondhand books in it – surely the most unlikely library building in the world!

A rare Brentwood privy – and a most unlikely library building!

[12]

LOOS LIVING

And now, for a last look back down the years and down the
garden to the old Essex privy, we are indebted to Ruth Proud.

Years ago, in the good old days, we didn't have no loos,
A little hut in the garden is what we had to use.
We had a great big bucket beneath a wooden bench so long
And I must admit that usually we also had a pong.

A hole worn smooth by years of use was just above the pail
And squares of paper on a string were hanging on a nail.
Sometimes there were smaller holes, especially for kids
And if you were posh the holes would be covered by some lids.

When you paid a visit you lost all modesty
'Cos all could see you take that path – there was no secrecy.
Often neighbours' privies would be built quite close together,
So if you were really friendly you could chat about the weather.

In winter you wore hats and coats, but all the bare bits froze,
And in the summer there were flies which settled on your nose.
There were crawly things and spiders, and things that bit
    your bottom,
So you passed the time quite happily trying hard to swat 'em.

Once a week Dad had the job of emptying the bucket;
Although I'm sure he'd like to, there was no way he could
    duck it.
He'd dig a hole then fill it up with eyes so full of pain,
'Cos he had to put the bucket back to be filled up once again.

Now we have baths and showers and loos and coloured toilet
  rolls,
No more buckets or newspaper or wooden seats with holes.
Although those primitive privies were a long way from
  perfection,
When we look back at childhood we think of them with
  affection.

An evocative picture by Don Wellman of two privies, survivors of four, built in
pairs, back to back, which served a row of cottages deep in the Essex
countryside.

A PRIVY BY ANY OTHER NAME

Convenient code-names as used from the 14th century to the present day.

Aster-room
Auntie's
Aunt Jones (1870–1905)
Backhouses
Bog
Boggard (1552)
Boghouse
Bombay
Bumby
Can
Certain room
Chamber of Commerce
Chapel-of-ease
Cloakroom (20th century)
Closet (1869)
Convenience (19th century)
Crapphouse
Dike, Dyke (19th century)
Dubbix
Dubs
Dunnekin
Garden loo
Garderobe
Geography of the house
George
Go for a Jimmy (Riddle)
Gong, Gonghouse
Go to see a man about a dog
Grot
Heads

Holy of holies
Honk
House of Commons (mid
    15th century)
House of Office (1609)
Houses of Parliament
How's yer Father
Hum
Ivy house
Jakes, Jacques (1530s)
Jericho
Jerry-come-tumble (before
    1860)
John
Karzi
Klondike
Larties
Larty farty
Latrine (1642, military use)
Lav
Lavatory (1845)
Little girls' (boys') room
    (1944)
Little House
Long Drop
Loo (commonest middle
    class name, derived from
    l'eau or lieu)
Mrs Jones (c1860)
Necessary house (1611)

Newspaper house
Offices
Opportunity
Out (up, down, round) the
    back
Pay a visit
Place (where you cough)
    (c1920)
Privy (from 1375)
Proverbial
Reading room
Sammy
Shant(y)
Shithouse, Shittus
Siege (-house) (c1440)
Slash (house)
Small house, smallest room
Sociable
Stool (1542)
Thinking house
Throne room (20th
    century)
Thunderbox
Toilet (from USA)
Water closet
Wee house
Wha'd'y'ma'callit
What's-its-name
Where the Queen goes on
    foot/sends nobody
Widdlehouse
Widdlystinks
Windsor Castle
You-know-where

ACKNOWLEDGEMENTS

I am grateful for *all* the help I received in my search for the privies of Essex. Some of my many kind contributors – people who went to particular lengths to make sure that I had all the information I needed – should, I feel, be mentioned by name. They are:

Judith Abbott, Mr and Mrs N. Andrew, Mr C. Balm, Mr and Mrs Beaumont, Derek Bircher, an old friend, Mr and Mrs Bunting of Rye Farm, Terry Cassels, Jill Cowley of Park Farm, Norman Croft, Mr and Mrs Doggett, Jim Foster, Mr E. Hurst, Angela Parker, Ruth Proud and Don Wellman, Mr and Mrs Richter, Mr S. Tinworth, Ken Walker, friend in all things Essex, Alan Weedon and Len Wyatt.